Read-About® Health

Pinkeye

By Sharon Gordon

Consultants
Nanci R. Vargus, Ed.D.
Assistant Professor
Literacy Education
University of Indianapolis
Indianapolis, Indiana

Jayne L. Waddell, R.N., M.A., L.P.C.
School Nurse/Health Educator/Lic. Professional Counselor

℗ Children's Press®
A Division of Scholastic Inc.
New York Toronto London Auckland Sydney
Mexico City New Delhi Hong Kong
Danbury, Connecticut

Designer: Herman Adler Design
Photo Researcher: Caroline Anderson
The photo on the cover shows a doctor checking a girl's eyes.

Library of Congress Cataloging-in-Publication Data

Gordon, Sharon.
  Pinkeye / by Sharon Gordon.
    p. cm. — (Rookie read-about health)
  Includes index.
  Summary: Simple text explains what pinkeye is, how it spreads, and
  common treatments for this eye infection.
    ISBN 0-516-22583-9 (lib. bdg.)   0-516-27396-5 (pbk.)
    1. Conjunctivitis—Juvenile literature. [1. Conjunctivitis. 2. Medical
  care.] I. Title. II. Series.
    RE320 .G67 2003
    617.7'73—dc21   2002015125

Good morning!

It is time to open your eyes.
Today, that is hard to do.

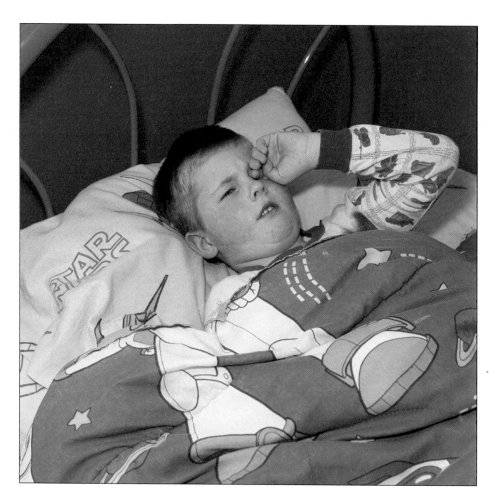

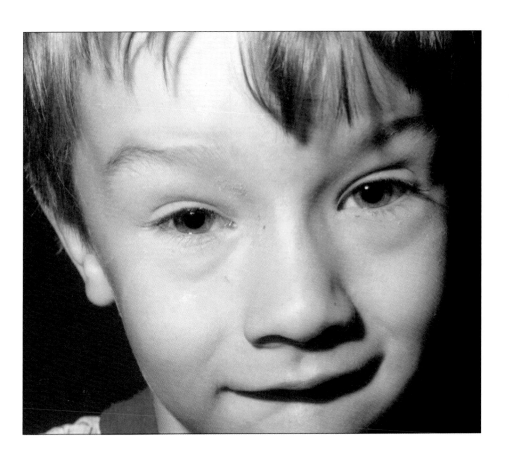

Your eyes feel sticky
and itchy. They are
puffy and sore.

It feels like there is something stuck in them.

You rub and rub, but it does not help.

It makes them itch even more!

Take a look at your eyes.

Do the white parts look pink or red?

You may have pinkeye.

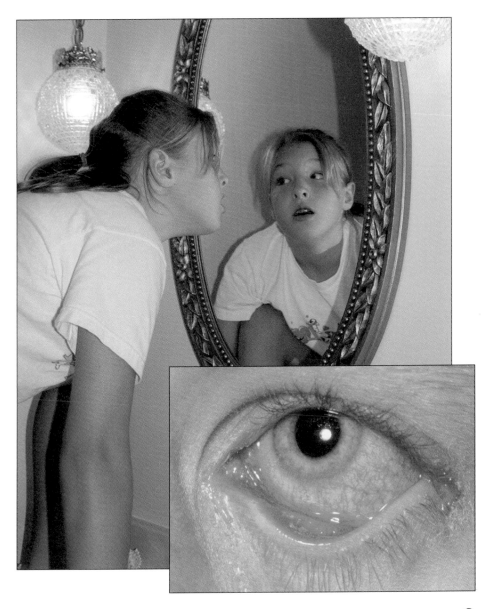

9

Your eyes have a
clear covering.

Sometimes, germs can get into the covering. They cause an *infection*.

Your body tries to fight
the germs.

It sends special cells to
your eyes.

These are called white
blood cells.

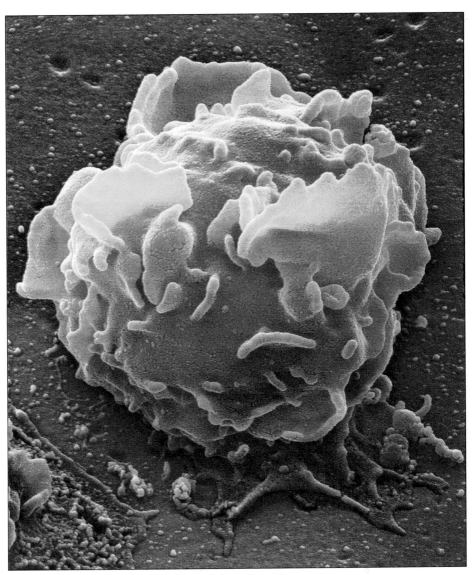

Close-up view of a white blood cell

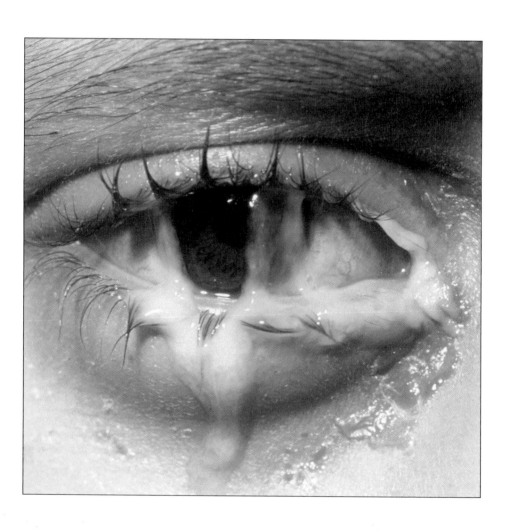

14

The white blood cells
create pus.

That is why your eyes
feel sticky.

Pinkeye is very common.

It is easy to catch from someone else.

It is also easy to give pinkeye to someone else.

18

Tell your parents if you think you have pinkeye.

They will help you clean out your eyes.

They will show you how to keep pinkeye from spreading to other people.

Try not to touch your eyes.

If you do, wash your hands right away.

Use warm, soapy water.

21

You will need your own towel. Otherwise you may spread the germs.

See a doctor to find out for sure if you have pinkeye.

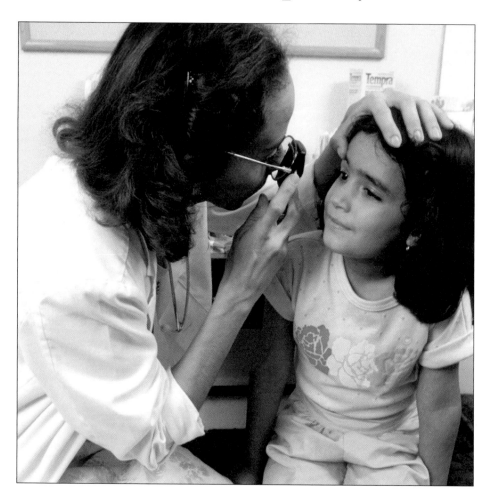

If you do, you will need
to take medicine.

It may be eyedrops. It may
be a special cream that you
put on your eyes.

You will need to stay
home from school for
a day or two.

The medicine works quickly
to stop the itchiness.

That feels so much better!

In about a week, the
pinkeye will be gone.

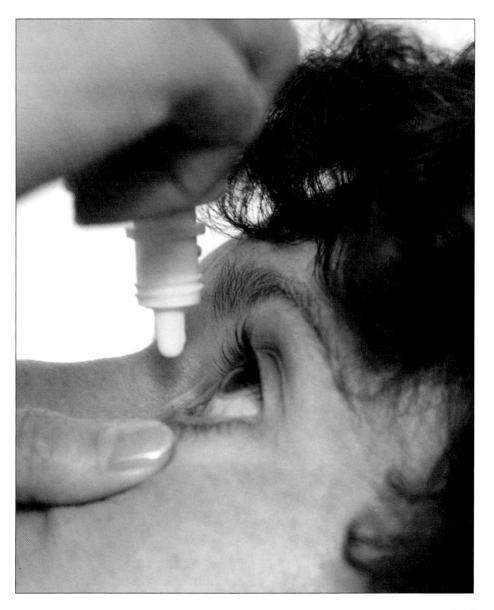

Good morning, bright eyes!

Words You Know

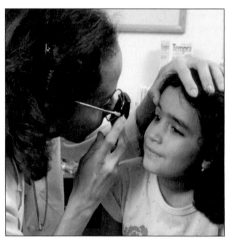

doctor

eyedrops

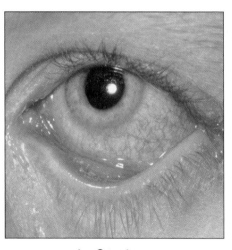

infection

itchy

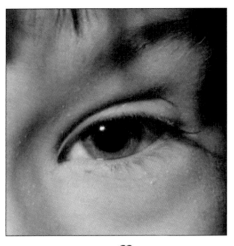

puffy

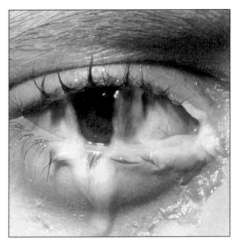

pus

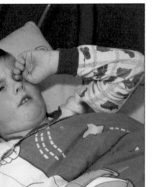

rub

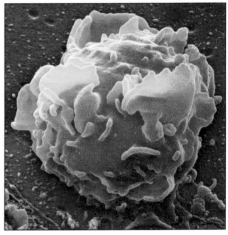

white blood cell

31

Index

catching pinkeye, 16

clear covering of eyes, 10, 11

cream, 25

doctor, 24

eyedrops, 25

eyes, 4, 5, 8, 10, 12, 15, 19, 20, 25, 29

germs, 11, 12, 23

infection, 11

itchy eyes, 5

medicine, 25, 26

puffy eyes, 5

pus, 15

sticky eyes, 5, 15

washing hands, 20

white blood cells, 12, 15

About the Author

Sharon Gordon is a writer living in Midland Park, New Jersey. She and her husband have three school-aged children and a spoiled pooch. Together they enjoy visiting the Outer Banks of North Carolina as often as possible.

Photo Credits